ANIMAL ARCHITECTURE

ANIMAL ARCHITECTURE

by Jennifer Owings Dewey

ORCHARD BOOKS • NEW YORK

Orchard Books
A division of Franklin Watts, Inc.
387 Park Avenue South
New York, NY 10016

Manufactured in the United States of America
Book design by Jean Krulis

10 9 8 7 6 5 4 3 2 1

The text of this book is set in 15 pt. Meridien.
The illustrations are pencil on vellum.

Library of Congress Cataloging-in-Publication Data
Dewey, Jennifer.   Animal architecture / Jennifer Owings Dewey.   p.   cm.   Summary : Explores the
kinds of habitats animals build for themselves.   ISBN 0-531-05930-8.   ISBN 0-531-08530-9 (lib. bdg.)
1.   Animals—Habitations—Juvenile literature.   2.   Habitat (Ecology)—Juvenile literature.
[1.   Animals—Habitations.]   I.   Title.   QL756.D48 1991   591.56'4—dc20   90-43010   CIP   AC

This book is for Ivan,
who is an architect
and a friend.

CONTENTS

INTRODUCTION

For a long time I have been fascinated and mystified by animals as builders. When I see a seashell, a honeybee hive, or a hummingbird's nest, I realize other animals besides ourselves are masons, carpenters, weavers, carvers, diggers, and structural engineers. They work in groups or alone. They use their jaws, teeth, beaks, legs, and claws to build homes and hiding places, food-catching traps and storage rooms. All animals have similar reasons for building—adapting their environments to minimize the dangers in their worlds.

Prairie dogs excavate tunnel systems underground, working with family members. When the prairie dogs move away, snakes, owls, and roadrunners move into the tunnels.

Termites construct forty-foot mounds, known as termitaries, that house millions of termites. They build with dirt, droppings, and saliva.

The male weaverbird works tirelessly for weeks braiding and twisting grass, twigs, and leaves into a snug hanging nest—a home for a new generation of weaverbirds.

Many birds and animals build by combining materials they gather from their surroundings. Some use substances made in their bodies, spinning webs and cocoons, or building protective shells with minerals absorbed from water. A tiny jumping spider on a mountainside devises a temporary shelter by spinning a silken web and anchor line. Microscopic animals absorb calcium from seawater and build hard shells around soft bodies.

The architecture of animals is often difficult for humans to see. Some of the most exciting constructions, those made by insects, are completely hidden from view.

A million and a half different kinds of animals live on the earth, and thousands of these create dwellings for themselves—or adapt existing ones. These dwellings range from the self-made castles of microscopic organisms to the complex structure of a honeybee hive to the relatively expansive comfort of a beaver lodge. A closer look at these often beautiful and innovative structures can reveal the scope of what and how animals build.

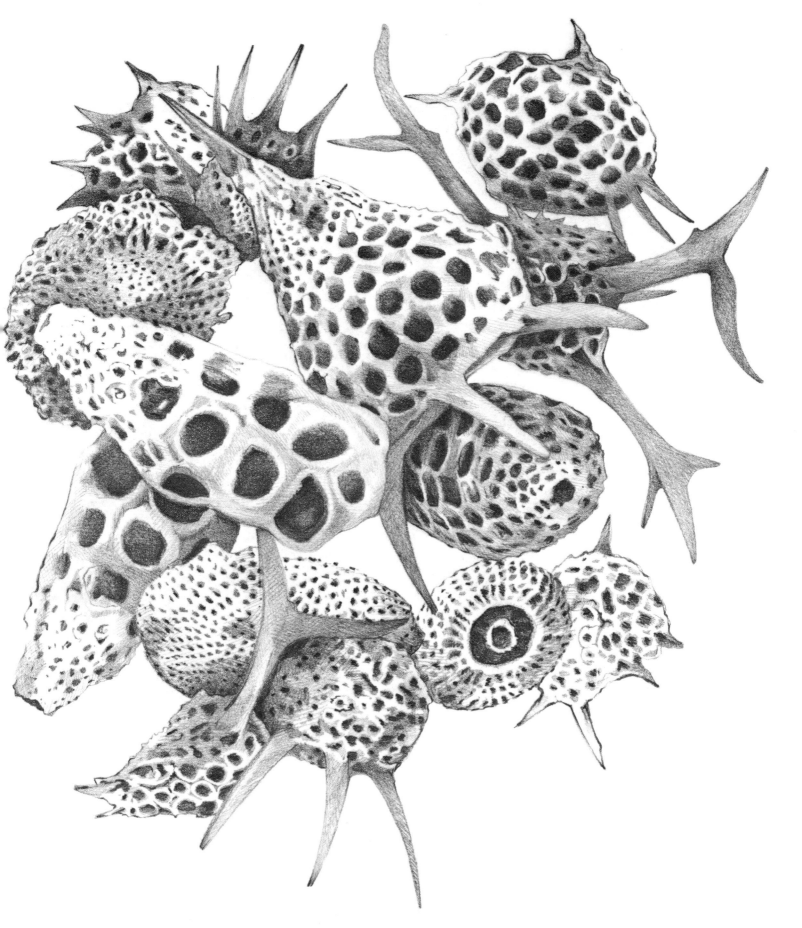

RADIOLARIANS

Countless numbers of nearly invisible, one-celled animals called plankton live in the oceans of the world. Because plankton need sunlight to live, they congregate near the ocean surface where there is an abundance of light. Radiolarians are one kind of the plankton that float and drift in warm seas. Like many other such animals, Radiolarians build protective shells around their soft bodies.

To construct shells, Radiolarians, like some other plankton forms, combine sand or minerals from water with secretions made in their bodies. Sand and minerals are their building materials; secretions are their cement.

Radiolarians absorb a mineral called silica and build shells that look like glass from it. These shells can look like tiny helmets, bells with holes in the sides, or balls with spines sticking out. Radiolarians are incredibly small; twenty can sit on a pinhead and not touch each other.

Floating in a watery universe, radiolarians are swept through the sea by ocean currents. To eat, they poke arms of protoplasm through holes in their shells and capture animals and plants even smaller than themselves. After they die, their soft protoplasm dissolves into the sea, but their shells sink slowly to the sea bottom. Over the course of millions of years the shells accumulate, turning to rock. The White Cliffs of Dover are made of these shells—and rise 375 feet above the sea.

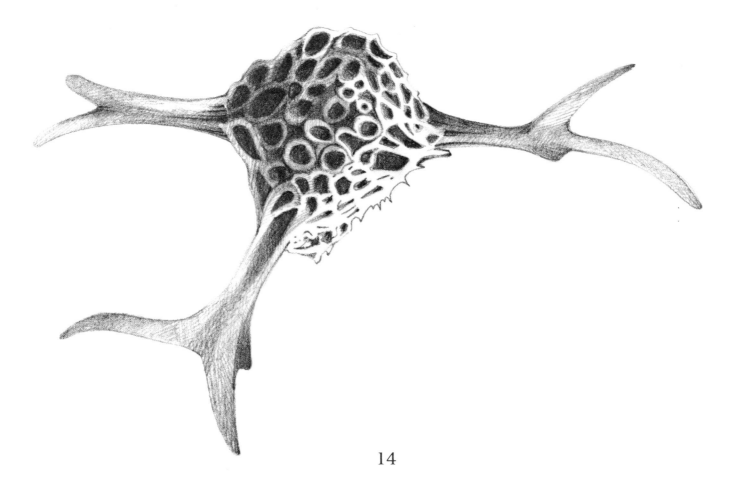

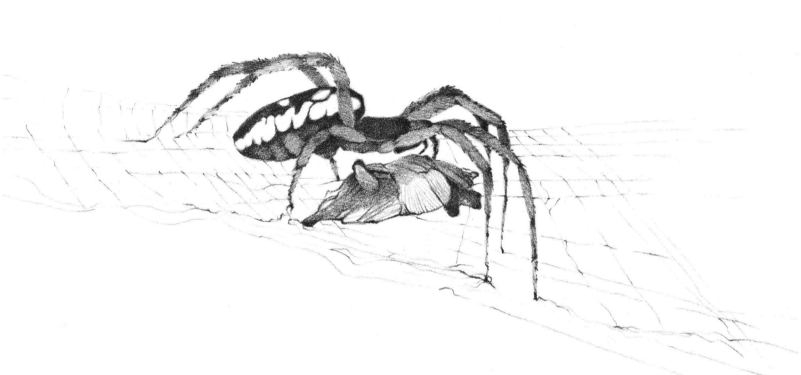

SPIDER SILKMAKERS

Spider silk has been used for centuries: to make nets for catching fish, to pack wounds, and to make the thin hairline sights on telescopes. People have learned that spider silk is one of nature's strongest fibers.

Silk is crucial to a spider's survival. It is used to snag and trap insects—the spider's primary prey. There are some kinds of insects that make silk in saliva glands inside

15

their mouths during larval stages. But spiders are unique in making silk throughout their entire lives.

Spiders are master silkmakers. The silk is made in glands of the spider's body. At the tip of its abdomen are spinnerets, tiny bumps with holes from which the silk emerges. Some spiders can spin up to seven or eight varieties of silk, each one for a particular purpose.

Orb weavers are spiders named for the round webs they spin. An orb weaver building a web runs up, down, and across a shimmery network of silk. The spider's silk glands produce exactly the kind of silk it needs. Dry silk is used for the outer radius of the web. The center is made with sticky threads that trap insects and hold them in place until the spider attacks. Orb weavers use tough, gluey silk to wrap their insect victims before injecting them with a paralyzing poison.

Some tropical orb weavers spin colored silk to disguise their presence on a web. The patterns they weave into their webs perfectly match the patterns on their bodies.

Another species of spider, the cobweb weaver, combs its silk using the bristles on its back legs. Combing makes the silk fuzzy and dense. This creates a messy-looking cobweb, often found under stairs or in woodpiles. Cobwebs tangle and trap the spider's six-legged insect prey.

''Trap-door spiders''—also called hairy mygalomorphs—make burrows in the ground with linings of soft silk and hinged lids of silk, sand, and saliva. The burrows are so well camouflaged that insects do not see them. Trap-door spiders wait in their lairs to jump out and grab a meal.

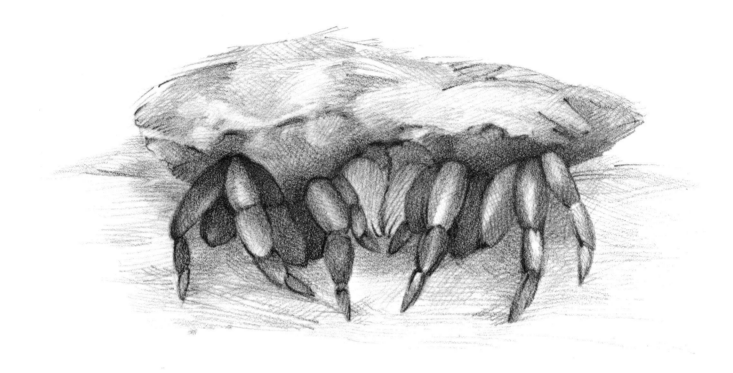

Spiders have developed other uses for silk, the wondrous fiber made in their bodies. "Spitting spiders" hurl masses of venom-soaked threads over unsuspecting insects. "Net-tossing" spiders hide in the grass and drop netlike webs on passing insects.

All but the most primitive spiders spin cocoons for their eggs. Most reserve their finest, softest silk to line these egg sacs and protect the delicate, tender spider eggs. Strong, waterproof silk is used for the outside of the egg sacs—making them durable and much more likely to survive, even under layers of winter snow. Spiderlings spend winter inside their egg sacs. Then they hatch in the spring, chewing their way free.

Spinning the egg sac is sometimes a spider's final silkmaking act, using up its silk glands forever. Without silk a spider dies, because it has no way to build traps and snares for insect prey.

BEES

In early spring I find myself listening for the whirring, whizzing, droning hiss of flying insects. I look for bees on the ground—those crawling stiffly from underground burrows after a winter of hibernating. If I am lucky I might see one launch itself into the air. To me the buzzy noise of bees always signals the end of winter.

SOLITARY BEES

There are more than twenty thousand species of bees, and 99 percent of these are "solitary"—they live alone. By contrast, social bees live in colonies organized around family groups: the queen, her daughters, and a few sons. Solitary bees come together only to mate. The males die soon after mating. Then the females, fertile and ready to lay eggs, gather pollen and nectar and begin to build egg cells for new broods of bees.

22

Solitary bees live in holes in the ground, in dead trees, or in worm-eaten, weathered wood. A female chooses a place for her egg cells—in the ground, in a tree, or in plant stalks and stems—that is near her own place of shelter.

23

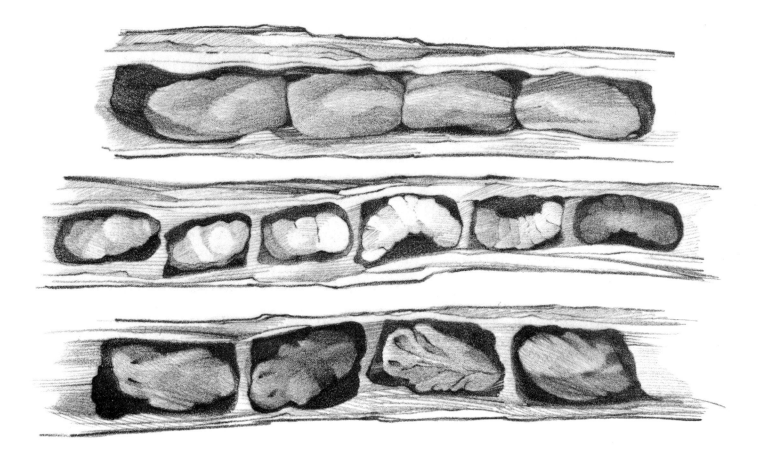

One kind of solitary bee—the leaf cutter—uses its legs and mouth to cut, roll, and twist leaves into thimble-shaped cells to hold each egg. Another solitary bee—the mason bee—chews a hole in tree bark or in the ground and lines it with a special mortar made of saliva, soil, pebbles, and pollen. Once an egg is placed in the cell, the mortar helps keep it warm and dry.

The developing bee larvae need food or they will die. Solitary bees often pack "bee bread"—a combination of

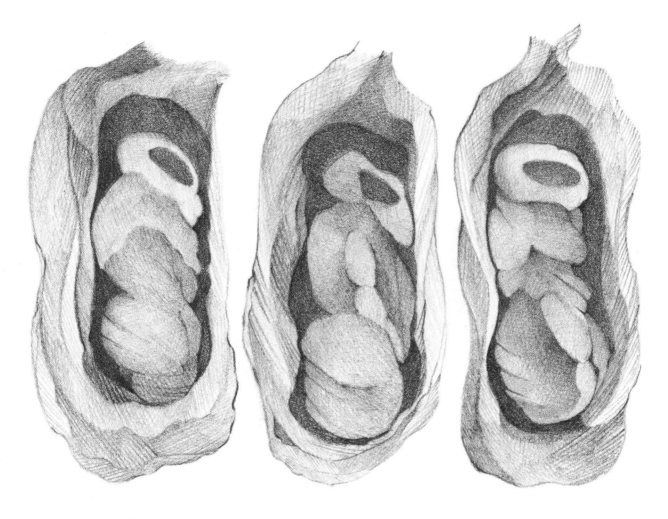

pollen, nectar, and saliva—into every cell for the larvae to eat as they grow. Solitary bees do not tend their cells, as social bees do. Instead they leave them to develop on their own using this store of food.

The larvae of solitary bees usually grow mature enough to leave their egg cells as adults by late summer. These new bees go into hibernation when winter comes. Then in the spring they crawl out of the ground, mate, and begin the life cycle of the solitary bee all over again.

BUMBLEBEES

Bumblebees are big, fuzzy, and yellow and black in color. Most people know bumblebees because of their size and their loud, humming buzz, but few will ever see a bumblebee's nest.

A bumblebee colony is a community of insects that are dependent on each other for survival. The ruler and founder of the colony is a fertile female—the queen. Under the queen are her infertile daughters—the workers. A few males develop in the colony. Their only function is to mate. After mating the males die.

In late summer new queens appear in the bumblebee colony. They mate and go into hibernation in the ground for the winter. When the warm spring weather returns, they emerge from hibernation and take to the air to look for a place to lay their eggs and begin new colonies of bumblebees.

A bumblebee queen newly out of the ground will find a place like an old mouse or mole hole or a crack in a log to build her nest. She manufactures wax inside her body, and it slides out from folds of skin on her belly.

To build a nest, the queen scrapes a smooth spot and lays down a sheet of wax to protect the future colony from dampness. Over this she spreads clumps of pollen gathered from flowers. Then on the pollen she lays a cluster of eggs. The queen applies a thin layer of wax over everything and for five days sits on top of the eggs to keep them warm.

When the eggs hatch, the larvae feed on the pollen. In seven days, the larvae pupate and spin cocoons of silk,

using silk glands inside their mouths. For ten more days they grow, until finally they emerge as adults—sterile females.

Flying from one spring flower to another, the queen gathers nectar. Back at her nest site, she has constructed a storage jar, or "honey pot," out of wax; she fills it with the nectar she gathers. She swallows and regurgitates the nectar several times, causing it to thicken, and in a few days it turns into honey. The queen feeds a few droplets of this rich honey to the larvae—or baby bees—in their cocoons.

If the queen is successful, she will have a thriving colony of female worker bees. These infertile daughters care for new eggs as they are laid. Workers feed the bee larvae. The queen lays more eggs, including eventually a few males, and thus the colony grows.

Bumblebees use deer fur, feathers, and spider silk to reinforce their wax. These materials are collected just the way pollen and nectar are, and carried to the nest under a bee's body, on its legs.

As summer ends, new queens develop in special cells in the colony. Winter cold will kill all members of the colony but these few queens, who mate before hibernating. New colonies depend on the reappearance of these queen bees the following spring, as they fly out and lay eggs in new nest sites.

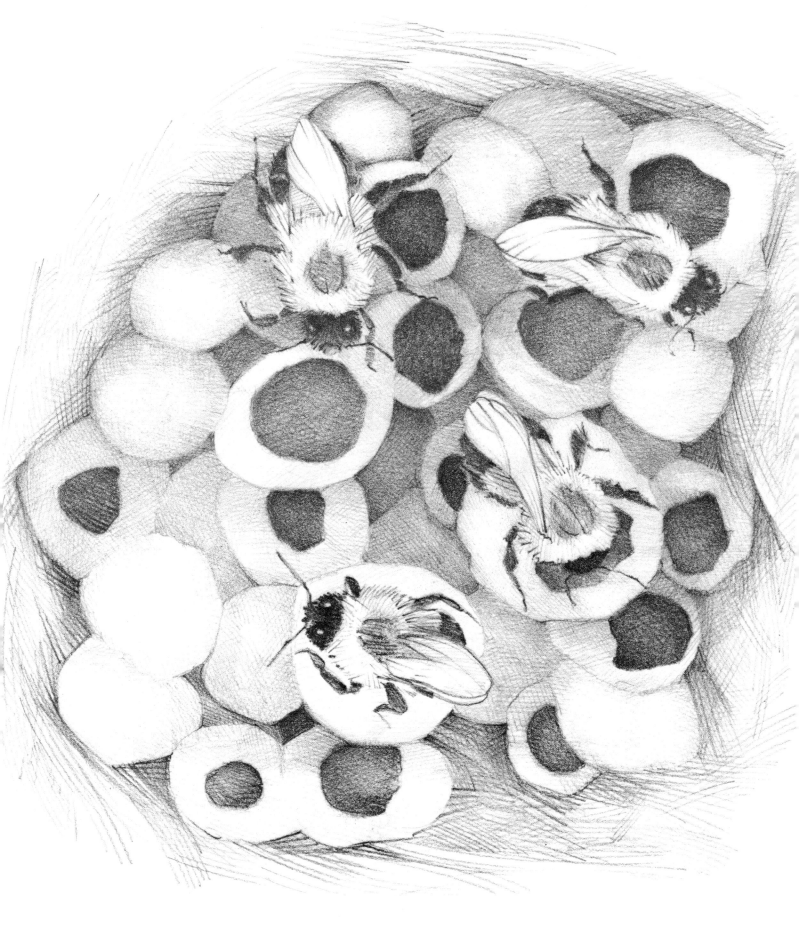

HONEYBEES

Human beings have long delighted in the sweetness of the honeybee's honey. Other bees make honey, but none produce it in such quantities as the honeybee. And no other bees survive winter's deadly freeze and still maintain their honey store. Honeybee hives are so well built that some last as long as thirty years.

A lot of bees die every winter from cold, but the death rate usually matches the birthrate. If the birthrate leads to overcrowding, a hive will divide; half the bees then swarm with a new queen to build a new hive. The remainder stay with the old queen in the original hive.

A swarm of bees looking for a new hive location mass in a dense ball around their queen. A honeybee's

31

wax glands work only if a bee is warm. Bunching together raises the body temperature of each bee. While bee scouts fly about looking for good nest sites, the swarm is preparing itself for wax-making.

Bees can communicate with each other by various methods, such as chemical signals. Bee scouts, flying back to the swarm, are able to provide information about nest sites. When a site is discovered all the bees will fly to it and begin to build.

The core of the hive is the comb, the portion used to shelter eggs and the growing baby bees. Honey is also stored in the comb. As wax flakes off the bees' bellies, they shape, knead, and soften it. This is how they begin to build the comb.

Working from the top down, bees construct cells in vertical rows. Each cell is built on a slant so the honey will not run out. Gravity-sensitive hairs on a bee's body tell it which way is up and which way is down.

A honeybee cell is a hexagonal prism—the most stable and efficient shape possible. There is no space between cells, and no need to build separate walls for any cell. When bees begin to build a hive they make just enough cells to start a brood. More cells are added as the new worker bees hatch out and the queen lays new eggs.

Many honeybees mix resin, or sap, with their wax after collecting it from flowers and trees. The addition of

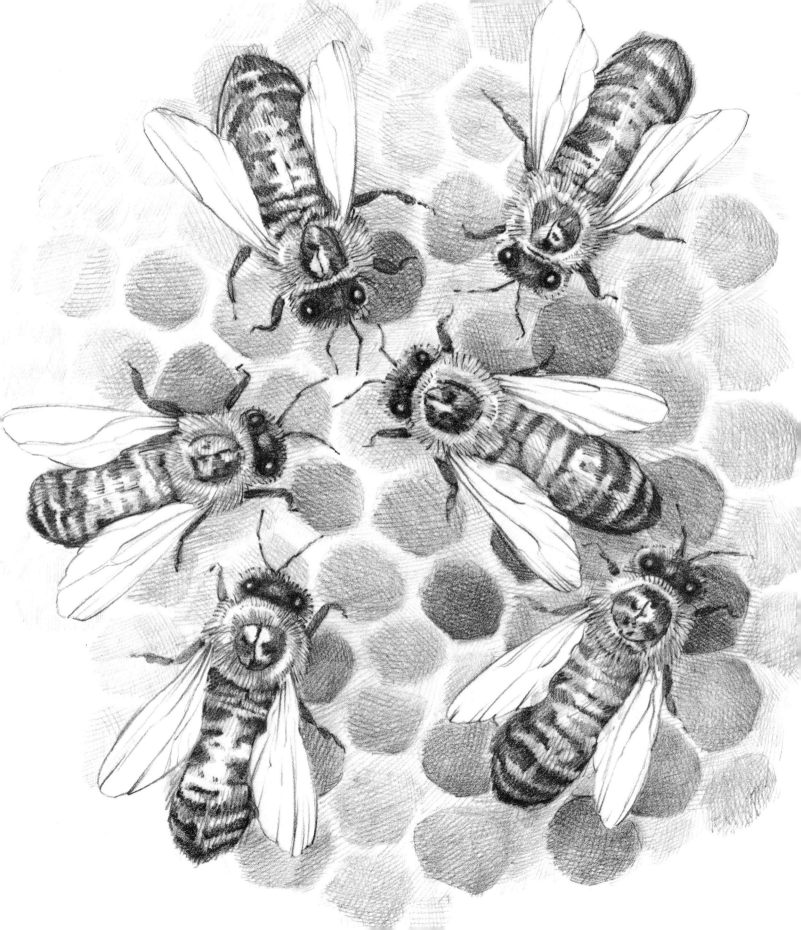

resin makes the wax stronger. Resin is also used to plug holes in the hive, to make it draft-free. Bees save energy and time by reusing and reinforcing their wax. Resin collected for hive repairs is carried on bristles, or "pollen-baskets," on a bee's back legs.

Life in a honeybee hive is constantly busy. The bees rest, but never sleep. No space is ever wasted. If cells are no longer needed for eggs, they are filled with nectar or pollen.

Healthy hives produce about two pounds of honey on a good day. The architecture of the hive and the division of labor among its forty to seventy thousand members account for the hive's success.

The work of the hive is divided among its members, according to each bee's age. Newly hatched bees are "nurse" bees; they feed the larvae and tend the cells. Two-week-old bees are storekeepers, guards, house-cleaners, and wax-makers; they keep the cells clean and filled with honey. They also guard hive entrances and make wax for new cells.

At three weeks a bee is old enough to become a forager, collecting pollen and nectar from flowers. A honeybee's stomach is about the size of a pinhead. It takes fifteen hundred trips to a flower to gather two tablespoons of nectar. The job is so demanding that foragers die of exhaustion after three weeks.

The few males that develop in the hive are called drones. Drones live short lives and produce no wax. Their only purpose is to fly on nuptial, or mating, flights. And after mating they die. The extra males are evicted from the hive and meet a similar fate.

One of the mysteries of the honeybee hive is how the workers know to feed nothing but royal jelly to certain larvae. Those that are fed only this rich mixture of pollen and nectar will always become queens.

The number of queens that emerge from the cells in a hive depends on its overall size. New queens must either leave the hive or be faced with fighting the established queen to the death. Usually the new queens leave and attempt to start their own hives. Many will die of exposure. But a queen that survives may live up to seven years, producing millions of offspring.

TERMITES
Insect Civil Engineers

Termites living in northern climates are often found in houses and barns, eating away at wood and plasterboard—causing serious damage. A termite's important role in nature is to help break down organic matter. It is only when termites begin to eat the structures people have built that they are thought of as "pests."

Sometimes called white ants, termites are one of the earth's oldest insects. The mounds they build in tropical countries show their amazing abilities as civil engineers. Termitaries, or termite mounds, last hundreds of years and are home to millions of termites. Though small in stature, termites are mighty builders.

Termites live in highly organized colonies, with the

labors of the nest divided among its members. A termite's role is determined when it first hatches; it is fed various secretions from the mouths and bodies of other termites, and these feedings alter the termite's internal development. Some grow into reproductive adults, others into workers or soldiers.

Several times a year, often after a heavy storm, reproductive termites will swarm from their mounds and mate. Mated pairs then find a hole in the ground and start raising broods of eggs, forming the nucleus of a new colony. The first termites to be born are workers. Their

function is to build the nest, nurse the young, and collect food. Later the workers will raise the soldiers who defend the colony.

When there are enough workers, they begin to build a mound. A termite mound is a complex arrangement of rooms and passages—usually symmetrical—ventilated with shafts and ducts for air circulation. Worker termites mix their droppings with saliva, making a cement to plaster the walls of the mound and its outer surface. Plastering helps to control temperatures in the mound and maintain the water supply.

One room in the mound is the royal chamber, where the king and queen reside. A termite queen is an egg-laying machine, producing up to fifty thousand eggs a day. Her body swells to such a size that she cannot leave her royal room. The mound's passages are too narrow for her to fit through.

Some mound-building termites raise food in "fermentation" rooms. There the worker termites lay down plant material on spongy masses of their own droppings. The plants decay, rot, and mold; then a fungus begins to grow—one the termites can eat. Gasses from these rooms also provide heat for the mound. On especially cold days worker termites carry eggs and larvae from one room to another, seeking the warmest spots.

Termites rarely leave their mounds, except to collect food at night and when swarming. Openings to the outside world are not much wider than the width of a single termite. Most termites have no eyes, because they live in darkness and have no need to see. Termites do need to drink, however. And to find water they often dig fifty, sixty, or one hundred feet into the earth to reach ground water.

A termitary, with as many as ten million termite residents, runs so smoothly that it acts like a single organism—a universe unto itself.

BIRDS

Sitting in the woods, watching a bird build a nest, I have usually assumed it is the female I am seeing. But in fact it is more often the male. Even when the male and female bird share in raising their young, the males commonly take charge of building and repairing the nest.

Birds build nests to shelter eggs and to provide soft places for growing chicks. Some birds go beyond this, creating elaborate architectural wonders that serve as hideouts, retreats from bad weather, breeding rooms, incubators, and roosting spots.

THE PENDULINE TITMOUSE

The male penduline titmouse, a bird common in Asia, Africa, and Europe, weaves a hanging, bag-shaped nest so durable that children can wear them as slippers or use them as purses. These titmouse nests are attached to twig ends and swing freely, making them nearly inaccessible to predators.

Fluttering around a branch, using his beak to carry and weave, a titmouse coils fine strands of plant material over and under, building up a dense mesh. Working for two or three weeks, the titmouse knits and interlocks everything until his nest is finished. Then he adds fluffy, fuzzy seed hairs from willows and poplars to make a soft lining.

Through an opening on one side of this hanging nest the titmouse can come and go. A titmouse will sometimes build two apparent openings—a false entry leading to a blind chamber to foil predators, and a true entrance to the nest cavity. The true entry is difficult to detect since the parent closes it after entering.

When the nest is complete the male searches for a mate. After he finds one, the pair will raise several families of chicks in the hanging nest.

WEAVERBIRDS

Weaverbirds live in large colonies in the African bush, or backcountry. Thirty to sixty birds may build nests in a single tree.

To build a nest, a weaverbird uses palm fronds, tree leaves, grasses, roots, and vines. The nests are built section by section. The weaverbird's beak and feet are his tools. These birds know how to knot and tie, so their nests are

flexible and strong. The tops are closed, and an opening is left on one side.

It takes weeks for a weaverbird to finish a nest. Not all nests are alike, because different weaverbirds use different materials and designs. After completing a nest, the male tries to win a mate. Males who are unable to find mates destroy their nests and begin new ones. Among weaverbirds the best nest wins the female.

OVENBIRDS

The ovenbird of Central and South America builds a nest that looks like a tiny baker's oven. Males and females, working in pairs, find a good source of clay for nest building. Using their feet for carrying, they transport more than two thousand miniature lumps of clay to the nest site. Nests are built on rock walls or the walls of houses and barns. Some ovenbirds build nests on the walls of caves. A nest may weigh sixty times the weight of a single ovenbird.

For ovenbirds, nest building begins in the winter, when the seasonal rains make the clay soft. By skillfully manipulating the clay with their beaks and feet, they sculpt small, ovenlike nests. One interior wall of clay is added to make nests stronger. To shape the insides of their nests, ovenbirds sit in them when the clay is wet, rubbing their bodies against the walls, molding the nest to a perfect fit. The clay is reinforced with grass, feathers, or fur. Still, ovenbird nests are fragile and can be used only once.

THE TAILORBIRD

To build nests, birds may work as weavers, potters, carpenters, or basket-makers. One little bird actually sews up his nest with a needle and thread.

The male tailorbird, who lives in China, India, and Southeast Asia, builds the nest. He uses his beak as a needle. For thread he uses spider silk or the fibers of tree bark. First he finds a leaf he likes, then punches holes along each edge of the leaf. The thread is pulled through each hole and knotted to keep it from slipping. Then the leaf is drawn together, just like a shoe being laced up.

To make the nest bigger, tailorbirds will sew two or more leaves together. Before setting out to find a mate, a tailorbird lines his little green house with sheep's wool or plant down. The tailorbird's nest is difficult to see because it looks so much like every other leaf in the tree.

SWIFTLETS

For centuries Chinese people have collected the hardened nests of swiftlets and made soup with them. They consider the nests a rare treat. These nests are made with one of the oddest building materials of all—the swiftlets' own saliva.

When mating and nest-building time comes, the saliva glands of swiftlet pairs swell to twice their normal size. A pair will choose a spot on a rock wall, often inside a cave, flying again and again to the same spot. Each time they leave a droplet of saliva. This gluey, threadlike substance hardens quickly. Bit by bit, layer by layer, a rim of saliva is raised on the rock. As it grows the swiftlets sculpt and shape it to make their nest.

Grass, leaves, and insect bits may be added to strengthen the nest. Swiftlets are highly skilled flyers and often gather nesting material in midflight, scooping up seed hairs and grass shreds in their beaks.

TENT-MAKING BATS

I used to think of bats just as hairy little creatures that flutter about in the dark and hang from rafters. Some bats fit this description, but there are many different kinds, and a variety of ways bats may use to find shelter.

When scientists first saw incisions in the leaves of rain forest trees in Central and South America, they thought they were made by insects. Eventually they discovered that a small white bat, called Thomas's fruit-eating bat, made the cuts.

Picking out bigger, tougher, fan-shaped leaves, these bats chew slits in the veins branching from the leaf's main rib. The fibrous strands that hold the leaf together are left intact, but the slits cause the leaf to hang down in a

52

tentlike shape. The bats hook their tiny feet and claws to rough spots on the underside of the leaf, hanging protected from the sun, wind, and rain—nearly invisible to predators.

Tent-making bats prefer leaves with spines and prickles. They tuck their bodies into the spaces between the spines. This makes it difficult for snakes, a serious enemy of the bats, to get at them.

Some mother bats carry their single baby, called a pup, to a night roost, and leave it there while they search for food. At the end of the night each baby is retrieved and carried to a day roost, where it can be with its mother.

Pairs usually live alone. But sometimes males with harems of females live as a commune under one big leaf tent.

THE HARVEST MOUSE

Rats and mice will build nests almost anywhere, in nooks, cracks, crevices, and other out-of-the-way corners—hoping to find a haven safe enough to raise babies. They collect fur, feathers, plant down, and leaf litter for their nests, using sharp teeth and claws to shred, rip, and chew these materials. Mice will sometimes bed down in a dresser drawer along with somebody's clothes.

One of the sturdiest, most elaborate and carefully assembled nests built by a mouse in the wild is the woven nest of the harvest mouse.

Measuring four inches from nose to tail-tip, the harvest mouse is one of the world's smallest mice. It climbs about among stems and stalks in meadows, marshes, and fields of oats, swinging from place to place on its tail. Harvest mice feed voraciously on seeds and also eat insects.

To build a nest, a harvest mouse uses both hands to grasp a few strands of grass. Pulling the grass to its mouth, the mouse draws each strand through its teeth, shredding it into long, skinny lengths.

The tiny creature weaves, laces, and knits blades of grass together to build a domed, basketlike nest with a single entry in the side. As a finishing touch, the harvest mouse lines the nest with spider silk, plant down, and flower petals, creating a soft bedding for the baby mice.

It is the female harvest mouse who weaves and builds the nest. Males make loosely thrown together sleeping mats and abandon them each morning. The males never stay in one place very long.

Litters of baby harvest mice are lively, bouncing creatures. After one litter of young a nest cannot be used again, because it is beyond repair. Harvest mouse mothers build new nests when more babies are on the way. A harvest mouse may produce three or four litters in a year.

PRAIRIE DOGS

Walking out on the prairie on a hot summer day I some-times catch sight of a fat, short-tailed animal standing on its hind legs, peering into the distance—a prairie dog. Prairie dogs are burrowing rodents, sixteen inches long including the tail. Looking further you might see two more prairie dogs, or twenty, or two hundred.

Prairie dogs are found in Central and North America.

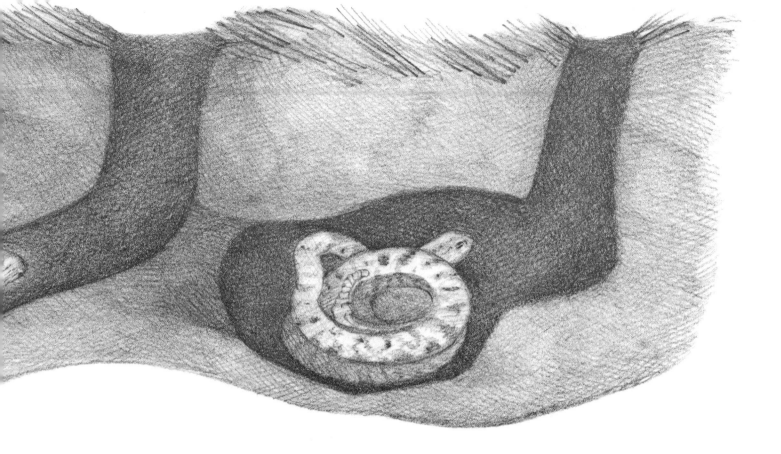

They live in "towns" excavated underground, colonies of hundreds of individuals. By living underground, prairie dogs find shelter from storms and predators. Hawks, badgers, falcons, and coyotes all prey on them.

Using their paws and noses to dig with, prairie dogs make vertical entrance holes leading to passages, tunnels, and rooms. In some of the underground rooms are stored grasses and weeds for food. Other rooms are for sleeping. Nursery and latrine chambers branch away from the main tunnels. Near the burrow openings prairie dogs dig out wide places where they can turn around.

With the dirt from their excavations, they create volcano-shaped mounds of hard-packed earth around burrow openings. The mounds serve as lookout posts to watch for predators and help prevent flooding in times of heavy rain.

A prairie dog town is a series of neighborhoods—each one made up of a family group. When two prairie dogs from the same neighborhood meet, they greet by rubbing noses, or "kissing." Pups rub their mother's face with their paws, begging to be nuzzled.

On warm summer days prairie dogs leave their burrows and scamper playfully about on "streets"—paths and runways on the surface. They whistle and call back and forth, grooming, eating, and sunbathing. In winter they hibernate deep in the ground, living on stores of dried grass.

Sometimes a bull snake takes up residence in a prairie dog tunnel. When this happens the prairie dogs wall off the section the snake is in and continue to use the remaining tunnels. Roadrunners and burrowing owls also move in. The roadrunners eat snakes, using the skins to line their nests. Nothing goes to waste in the wild.

BEAVERS

Once very early one morning I saw a beaver swimming in a marsh. The beaver saw me, slapped its tail hard on the water surface, and vanished. Beavers do their building at night. They usually sleep in the day, avoiding humans.

Beavers are rodents. Rodents have gnawing habits and big front teeth that never stop growing. A beaver's upper and lower front teeth meet, sharpening each one to a chisel edge. Beavers eat roots, bark, seeds, leaves, and saplings.

Working in family groups—a father, mother, and three or four offspring—beavers cut down trees for their dam. A beaver will stand on its hind legs and chew a groove in a tree trunk, under that another groove, and then another. Working its way around the trunk the beaver fells the tree.

Starting on the edges of the stream and working toward the middle, beavers will haul and stack trees, building up a dam. They ram strong branches into the stream bottom and stick smaller twigs in between them, making a tight mesh. Mud is dragged off the bottom of the stream and used to plug holes. Stones and mud are used to weigh sticks and branches down, keeping them in place.

When the dam is finished, beavers start their lodge, laying down a platform of sticks and saplings. A dome-shaped mound, twenty feet across, is raised. By gnawing

and chewing, beavers work a hole into the mound, creating their den. Mud is pulled off the stream bottom to serve as plaster for the outside of the lodge. Loose sticks piled on top allow for air circulation.

Shredded and chewed plants are scattered on the lodge floor to make a soft carpet. Water drains through the floor easily.

All entries and tunnels to the outside world are below the waterline. Beavers build a small ledge near one of the entry holes. There they let excess water drain off their fur before climbing up to the main room.

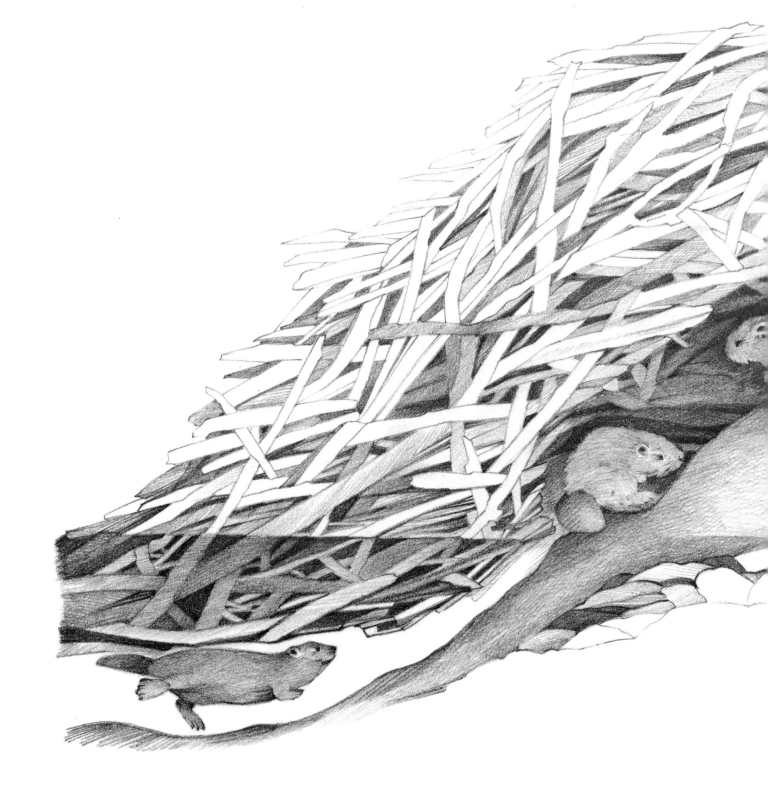

A beaver lodge is a dry island in a wet world. When ice covers the stream and winter snows drift over the land, the lodge may be invisible under a white blanket, but the beavers are safe and warm inside.

CONCLUSION

Humans build sheltering structures for themselves, first making plans, then making tools to build with. Insects and other animals use no formal plans and are naturally equipped with the tools and materials they need. Yet structures built by people are rarely as well suited to their needs as the honeybee hive is to a bee—or a mouse nest to a mouse. The extraordinary thing about animal architecture is how perfectly each dwelling suits its builder, how nicely every animal habitation fits its occupant.

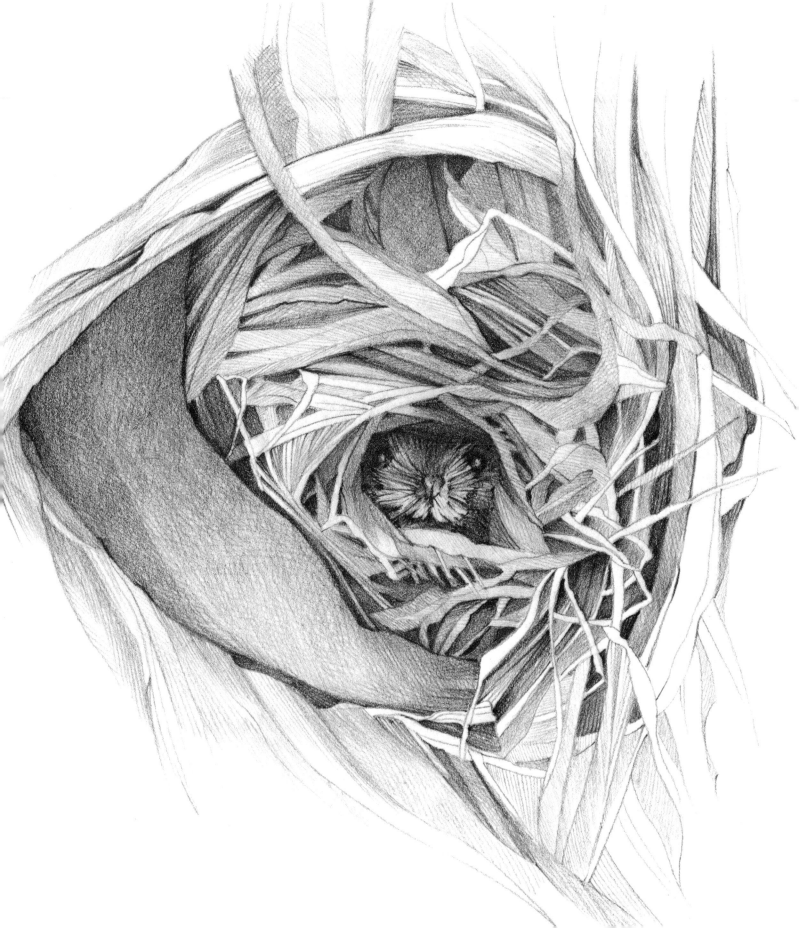

INDEX

Illustrations are indexed in **boldface**.